W9-ARO-312

A THOREAU GAZETTEER

A Thoreau Gazetteer

has been approved by the Editorial Board
as a supplement to THE WRITINGS OF
HENRY D. THOREAU, published by Princeton
University Press, and sponsored by
the National Endowment for the Humanities
and the Center for Editions of American
Authors of the Modern Language
Association.

A THOREAU GAZETTEER

by Robert F. Stowell

edited by William L. Howarth

PRINCETON UNIVERSITY PRESS

PRINCETON, NEW JERSEY

1970

COPYRIGHT © 1970 BY PRINCETON UNIVERSITY PRESS

ALL RIGHTS RESERVED

Published by Princeton University Press, Princeton and London

LCC: 69-56321

ISBN: 0-691-06156-4 (hardcover edition)

ISBN: 0-691-01315-2 (paperback edition)

First PRINCETON PAPERBACK Edition, 1974

PRINTED IN THE UNITED STATES OF AMERICA
BY PRINCETON UNIVERSITY PRESS

Sources of the maps in this book and acknowledgments of permission to reproduce them appear in the *Notes on the Maps* section following the text.

Contents

List of Illustrations

Acknowledgments

THE AUTHOR would like to acknowledge some of the many persons who have assisted him during his research on the *Gazetteer*. Special thanks must go to Professor Walter Harding, Secretary of The Thoreau Society, for his encouragement and counsel. Mr. John MacDonald and the members of the Department of Geography at the University of Canterbury offered both advice and space in their cartographic section. The Grants Committee of the University of New Zealand subsidized the cost of materials, and Miss Claire Cashmere, secretary to the English Department at Canterbury, cheerfully typed the manuscript. Professor Reginald Cook of Middlebury College and Mr. Leonard Kleinfield of New York City read parts of the manuscript and offered valuable comments. In addition to the University of Canterbury Library, numerous American libraries loaned books and photocopies of manuscript material. Of indispensable aid were the Concord Free Public Library, Concord, Massachusetts; the Alderman Library, University of Virginia, Charlottesville, Virginia; and the Middlebury College Library, Middlebury, Vermont. Everywhere his inquiries led him, from Canada to Virginia, and from Maine to Minnesota, the author encountered nothing but the highest degree of cooperation and interest. To those many persons not mentioned specifically, he sends his thanks for their kind and generous assistance.

ROBERT F. STOWELL, *Diamond Harbour, New Zealand*

THE EDITOR wishes to thank the following persons for supplying additional information and maps: Mr. Herbert C. Schultz, Huntington Library, San Marino, California; Mrs. Elizabeth R. Schubert, Alderman Library, University of Virginia; Mrs. Marcia E. Moss, Concord Free Public Library; Mrs. Lola L. Szladits, New York Public Library; and Mr. Walter W. Ristow, Library of Congress. Mr. Lawrence E. Spellman, Curator of Maps at the Firestone Library, Princeton University, offered valuable advice on cartographic matters. Mr. Lee Van Valkenburg and Mrs. Barbara Howarth labored nobly on an index to the *Gazetteer*; their work was supported by a grant from the University Committee on Research. Finally, Mrs. Eve Hanle, Mrs. Carol Orr, and Mr. Frank Mahood of Princeton University Press deserve special commendation for helping the editor bring this book to its final form.

WILLIAM L. HOWARTH, *Princeton, New Jersey*

Introduction

As we thus rested in the shade, or rowed leisurely along, we had recourse, from time to time, to the Gazetteer, which was our Navigator, and from its bald natural facts extracted the pleasure of poetry.

(W: i, 92)*

ALONG with botany and zoology, geography was clearly one of Henry Thoreau's life-long avocations. Most of his writings represent "the pleasure of poetry" that geography afforded, so the maps in this *Gazetteer* are presumably some of the "bald natural facts" that served as his raw material. The two elements, poetry and fact, mingled constantly in Thoreau's work and affected his personal behavior. That he was a stickler for accuracy and detail, for example, probably explains why he was a reliable surveyor. He enjoyed surveying, for no other job gave him the same freedom to set his own hours and places of business; yet when men misused his skills, the task often left him bitter and depressed. Landowners rarely understood the principles of surveying; they saw it only as a means of defining their property rights. This material view of the earth, Thoreau feared, might distort his own vision of nature:

> I have lately been surveying the Walden woods so extensively and minutely that I now see it mapped in my mind's eye—as indeed, on paper—as so many men's wood-lots . . . I fear this particular dry knowledge may affect my imagination and fancy, that it will not be easy to see so much wildness and native vigor there as formerly. No thicket will seem so unexplored now that I know that a stake and stones may be found in it. (*J*: x, 233)

Attraction and revulsion seem also to characterize his attitude toward maps. He must have been fascinated by them, for he never missed an opportunity to study a map and comment upon its accuracy. When he was traveling, maps were important guide-posts along the way; and when he was writing, they helped to provoke both his memory and thoughts. For example, while he was working on the essays later published as *Cape Cod*, he studied early maps of that region, some dating back to the seventeenth century. The French charts were by far the best, he concluded: "They went measuring and sounding, and when they got home had something to show for their voyages and explorations" (*W*: iv, 234). A map, then, was of value to Thoreau as an artifact of ex-

---

* All quotations are from *The Complete Writings of Henry David Thoreau* (Boston, 1906) 20 vols. The volumes are titled *Writings*, i-vi; and *Journal*, i-xiv. References are to *W* or *J*, by volume and page number.

perience; as he learned during his trip to Canada, it clarified "what would otherwise have been left in a limbo of unintelligibility" (*W*: v, 60).

Yet he was often frustrated by maps, partly because people did not read them properly, and partly because he feared they could not do otherwise. When he compiled a "list of things ill-managed" in society, one of his major grievances was the lack of a decent pocket-map of Massachusetts. A large map was available, but no one had ever thought to cut it into sheets suitable for a walker's use. The reason for this oversight, Thoreau complained, was that "Men go by railroad, and State maps hanging in bar-rooms are small enough" (*J*: ii, 396-70). In his view maps were not just a means for some commercial end; they served a spiritual purpose as well, and for that purpose they could never really be *large* enough. Often he was disappointed by the disparity between a map and his experience. The artifact did not seem adequate at all, because it failed to bring back the sights and smells of forest, seacoast, or mountain. This deficiency, of course, was inevitable, but still the conventions of map-making seemed partly responsible:

> How little there is on an ordinary map! How little, I mean, that concerns the walker and the lover of nature. Between those lines indicating roads is a plain blank space in the form of a square or triangle or polygon or segment of a circle, and there is naught to distinguish this from another area of similar size and form. . . . The waving woods, the dells and glades and green banks and smiling fields, the huge boulders, *etc.*, *etc.*, are not on the map, nor to be inferred from the map. (*J*: xiv, 228-29)

The ambivalence Thoreau felt toward surveys and maps also affected his attitude toward travel, the source of his geographical interests. During the course of his adult life he spent a considerable amount of time, energy, and even money on travel, yet he frequently condemned the practice as a waste of all three resources. He rejected many invitations to go abroad, arguing, as he did in *Walden*, that he could travel much in Concord. His sentiment seemed provincial to friends, but it actually had a broad philosophical basis. Thoreau believed that traveling, like surveying and map-reading, demanded a serious attitude, a proper spirit. Travel was not an escape from daily routine but an attempt "to get some honest experience of life," and thus it mattered little where or how far he went. Unlike most men, he wanted to live intensively; so every experience, including that of travel, had to be performed in a "simple, primitive, original manner . . ." (*J*: iii, 183-84).

Simplicity was the keystone of Thoreau's philosophy, so his application of that precept to travel was a sign of great esteem. When conducted simply and sincerely, travel became "as serious as the grave, or any part of the human journey," and it therefore required of the traveler "a long probation" in learning its skills (*W*: i, 325). Learning usually meant sacrifice, especially of creature comforts. When traveling, Thoreau avoided easy roads, carried little food, and wore only rough clothing because "the genuine traveler is going out to work hard, and fare harder,—to eat a crust by the wayside whenever he can get it. Honest traveling is about as dirty work as you can do, and a man needs a pair of overalls for it" (*W*: v, 31-32). His attitude may seem cranky to some, but others will find it appropriate. Thoreau demanded rudeness of the traveler because he foresaw the threat of America's urbanization. Travel could be an antidote to that poison, but only as long as its spirit matched the wilderness and not the city. As he noted in "Walking," the whole nation sought its freedom by traveling westward, but its only permanent freedom lay in preservation of the wild. All of Thoreau's books present that poetic message; the facts of geography were his means of presentation.

This *Gazetteer*, then, attempts to provide a geographical guide to the writings of Thoreau by including maps of three varieties: those drawn by Thoreau himself, those contemporary with his time, and those reconstructed from his accounts and other sources. The collection follows the sequence of his publication dates, beginning with *A Week* (1849) and ending with the *Journal* (1906). Accompanying the maps are texts which offer some explanatory material, as do the later supplementary notes. A chronological listing of his trips beyond the Concord area illustrates the range and variety of Thoreau's travels. Finally, an index correlates place names in Thoreau's writings with maps appearing in the *Gazetteer*.

The primary aim of this book is to give its readers an idea of the places Thoreau describes in his own books. The importance of those places will depend upon the readers' critical views of Thoreau. To those who read him literally, the maps will provide a convenient way of following his travels in Massachusetts, Maine, Canada, Cape Cod, Minnesota—locations that he actually visited in his life. To those who read him figuratively, the maps will depict symbolic rivers, ponds, mountains—settings that are the imaginative products of his art. Because the settings of Thoreau's books are synonymous with the places of his travels, readers who study this *Gazetteer* should find that it is a "Navigator" to both his life and art. If, in addition, this collection of "bald natural facts" contains some extractable poetry, credit is due largely to Thoreau.

NEW ENGLAND

Montmorency Falls
Quebec
MAINE

St. Lawrence River
14 - 17
CANADA

7 - 9
Mt Ktaadn
Moosehead Lake
Penobscot River
Kennebec River
Bangor

Montreal
Sorel River
St. John's

Rouses Pt.
Plattsburg
Lake Champlain
N. H.
Androscoggin River
Augusta
Camden

Burlington
VERMONT
Connecticut River
Mt. Washington
Bath
Monhegan Is.

NEW YORK
Mt. Killington
Newfound Lake
Lake Winnipiscogee
Saco River
Portland

Ludlow
Mt. Kearsarge
Bellows Falls
Mt. Monadnock
Merrimack River
Atlantic Ocean

Albany
Keene Troy
Brattleboro
Mt. Greylock
Fitchburg
MASS
Concord
4 - 6
18 19

CATSKILL MOUNTAINS
Pittsfield
Worcester
Boston

Springfield
Taunton
Plymouth
10-13
Sandwich
Hyannis

Hartford
Providence
CONN.
New Bedford
R.I.
Nantucket

NEW JERSEY
Hudson River
New Haven
New London
Naushon I.

New York
Long Island
N

Staten Island
Fire Is.

Perth Amboy

Philadelphia

0   30   60

46°
44°
42°

72°   70°

Thoreau's Travels

⚜ MAP ONE ⚜

WITH the exception of his Minnesota journey, this map represents all of Thoreau's travels between the years 1836 and 1861. The routes of his most important trips—those of several weeks' duration—are indicated, while the numerals refer to succeeding maps in the *Gazetteer*. The map was drawn from sources contemporary with Thoreau's time, but the spelling of place names follows Thoreau's own usage; e.g., "Plattsburg" for Plattsburgh.

As this map indicates, travel was a fundamental part of Thoreau's life. Lecturing took him over most of eastern Massachusetts, surveying brought him south to New Jersey, while curiosity—and later, the need for convalescence—drove him north to Quebec and west to Minnesota. Ten years of field trips, of course, gave him an indelible knowledge of the sixty square miles surrounding Concord. Other writers of the day might have ranged more widely, but few shared the depth of Thoreau's affection for travel: "Our life should be so active and progressive as to be a journey" (*J*: III, 240).

1

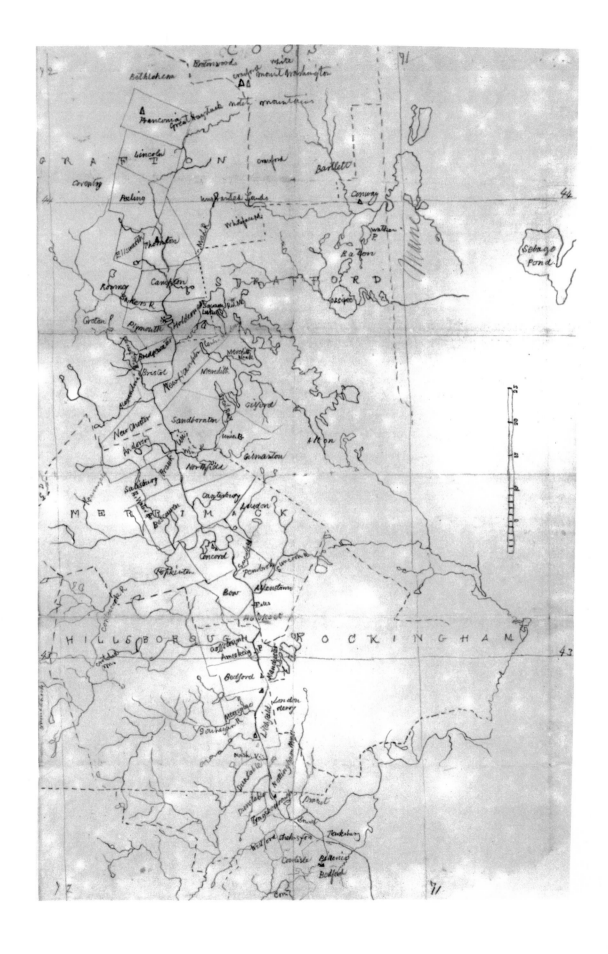

A Week on the Concord and Merrimack Rivers
❧ MAP TWO ❧

DRAWN by Thoreau himself, this map depicts the route of his first long journey, a voyage up river with his brother John in the late summer of 1839. Scaled originally at an eighth of an inch per mile (approx. 1:500,000),* the map extends from Concord, Massachusetts in the south (abbreviated "Con") to New Hampshire's White Mountains in the north. Thoreau represented the brothers' nightly camping spots with small triangles, or tents, at the following locations: Billerica, Tyngsborough, Nashville, Bedford, Hooksett, and Concord, New Hampshire. This part of the journey was by boat; it took six days to complete—from Saturday, August 31 to Thursday, September 5.

For the next six days, the Thoreaus traveled alternately by foot and stage. According to the triangles they camped overnight at Thornton, Franconia, Crawford Notch, Mt. Washington, Conway, and Concord, New Hampshire. They returned to Hooksett on Thursday, September 12, retrieved their boat, and by the following evening were home again in Concord. Thoreau has not dated his map, but the amount of detail indicates that he drew it not long after the trip.

* Representative fractions indicate the ratio of measurement between a map and the earth.

On the Concord banks, a river boat and American bittern. Photograph by Herbert W. Gleason.

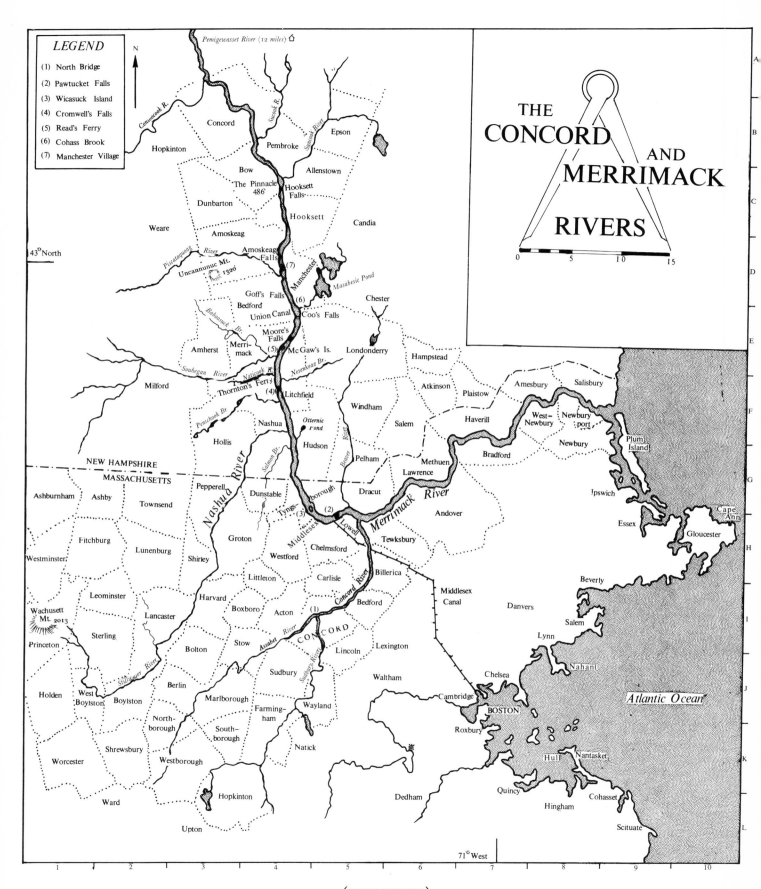

LEGEND

(1) North Bridge
(2) Pawtucket Falls
(3) Wicasuck Island
(4) Cromwell's Falls
(5) Read's Ferry
(6) Cohass Brook
(7) Manchester Village

THE
CONCORD
AND
MERRIMACK
RIVERS

0   5   10   15

Pemigewasset River (12 miles)

Contoocook R.

Concord

Hopkinton

Suncook River

Epson

Pembroke

Allenstown

Bow

The Pinnacle 486'

Hooksett Falls

Dunbarton

Hooksett

Weare

Amoskeag

Candia

43° North

Piscataquog River

Amoskeag Falls

(7)

Uncannunuc Mt. 1326

Manchester

Goff's Falls

(6)

Masabesic Pond

Chester

Bedford

Union Canal

Coo's Falls

Baboosuck Br.

Moore's Falls

Amherst

Merri-
mack

(5)

McGaw's Is.

Londonderry

Hampstead

Souhegan River

Naticook R.

Nesenkeag Br.

Atkinson

Amesbury

Salisbury

Milford

Thornton's Ferry

(4)

Litchfield

Windham

Salem

Plaistow

Haverill

West-
Newbury

Newbury
port

Pentucket Br.

Nashua

Otternic
Pond

Hudson

Beaver River

Pelham

Methuen

Bradford

Newbury

Plum
Island

Hollis

NEW HAMPSHIRE

MASSACHUSETTS

Lawrence

Ipswich

Ashburnham

Ashby

Townsend

Pepperell

Dunstable

Solmon Br.

Tyngs-
borough

Dracut

Merrimack River

Andover

Essex

Cape
Ann

Fitchburg

Lunenburg

Groton

(3)

(2)

Lowell

Tewksbury

Gloucester

Westminster

Shirley

Westford

Chelmsford

Beverly

Littleton

Carlisle

Billerica

Middlesex
Canal

Danvers

Salem

Wachusett
Mt. 2013

Leominster

Lancaster

Harvard

Boxboro

Acton

(1)

Concord River

Bedford

Lynn

Nahant

Sterling

Bolton

Stow

CONCORD

Lincoln

Lexington

Chelsea

Princeton

Assabet River

Waltham

Cambridge

Atlantic Ocean

Holden

West
Boylston

Boylston

Berlin

Sudbury

Sudbury River

Wayland

BOSTON

Roxbury

Hull

Nantasket

Worcester

Shrewsbury

Marlborough

Farming-
ham

Natick

Dedham

Quincy

Hingham

Cohasset

Ward

Westborough

South-
borough

Northborough

Hopkinton

Stillwater River

Upton

71° West

1   2   3   4   5   6   7   8   9   10

(MAP THREE)

A Week on the Concord and Merrimack Rivers

✦ MAP THREE ✦

THIS modern reconstruction offers a clearer view of the river voyage and of the surrounding country as well. Numerals appearing in parentheses correspond to important locations in *A Week*; a comparison of this map with Thoreau's original reveals to what extent he altered life (1839) for the sake of art (1849). The addition of boundaries for some towns not cited in *A Week* will aid readers of other writings, particularly the *Journal* and the collected *Correspondence*.

The cabin at Walden; an etching by W. H. N. Bicknell.

Walden

✦ MAP FOUR ✦

THOREAU first surveyed Walden Pond during the winter of 1846. He recorded his findings in a preliminary sketch and then shortly thereafter completed this fair copy. Mounted on cardboard, the map measures 16¼ by 20½ inches and contains a scale of ten rods to the inch (approx. 1:2,000). Thoreau has indicated features that will be familiar to readers of *Walden*: his "house" near the northwest cove, the Fitchburg Railroad tracks on the southwest, and the wooded peaks—one "about 85 ft. high"—of the north side. Readers should note that north in this map is toward the *bottom* edge.

Thoreau's notes below the drawing read as follows:

Soundings on BD, KJ & CM at intervals of ten rods; CN 15 rods; KL 300 & 200 feet on EF, GH, & shorter lines at intervals of 100 & occasionally of 50 and 25 feet measuring from E & G respectively. Distances on EF, BD,
GH, and short lines on the middle accurately measured—the others paced.
      s—soft bottom   h. hard
1 acre has over 100 feet of water upon it
2 acres over 99 [?]—7 acres over 80.

Area = 61 acres, 2 roods, 23 perches.
Circumference = 1.7 miles.
Greatest length 175½ rods
Greatest breadth 110½ "
Least   "   49½ "
Greatest unevenness observed on the bottom between
41 & 66 on EF, a descent of 25 feet in 50
Least unevenness between 53½ & 54½ on JK—one foot in 30 rods

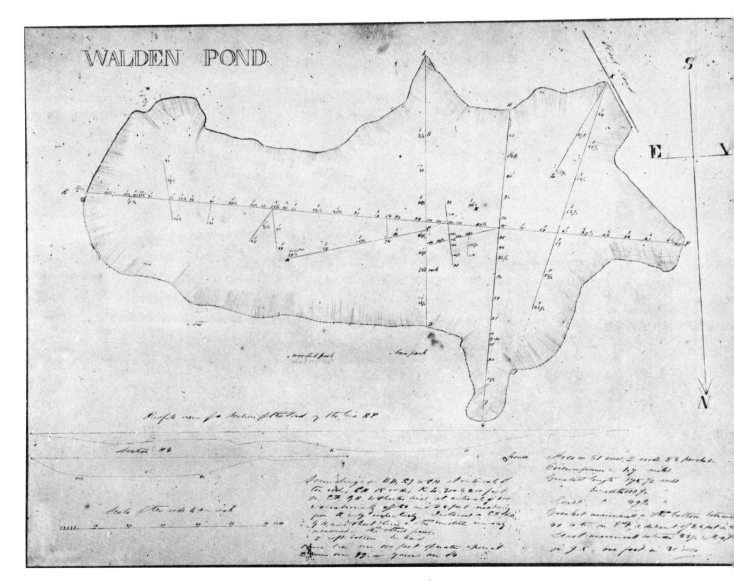

(MAP FOUR)

Walden Pond in May. Photograph by Herbert W. Gleason.

Walden

MAP FIVE

THOREAU probably drew this "Reduced Plan" in early 1854, just before he sent the *Walden* manuscript to press. His drawing served as a model for a lithograph of Walden Pond, dated 1846, that appeared in the first edition (see page 9). While this drawing obviously descends from Thoreau's fair copy of 1846, several differences between the two are apparent. The "Reduced Plan" is on a smaller scale, forty rods to an inch (1:7,

7

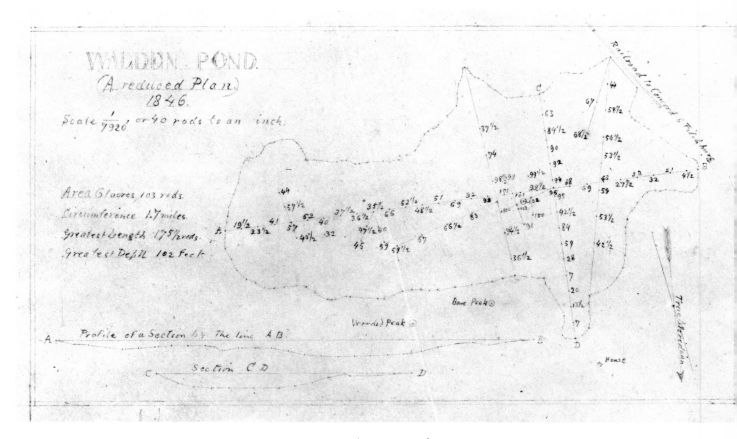

(MAP FIVE)

920); and Thoreau simplified matters for reader and lithographer alike by printing fewer soundings on the base lines. Only four reference points appear; his original EF and AD have become AB and CD. Angles of the baselines differ in the two maps, probably because Thoreau drew his survey from magnetic north while north on this drawing is a "True Meridian." As in the original, north continues to appear toward the *bottom* edge. The lithographer made no alterations in his copy of the drawing, except to substitute a more professional style of lettering.

The two drawings and the lithograph all indicate Thoreau's interest in establishing the geographical locale of *Walden*. Printed by the Boston firm of S. W. Chandler and Sons, the map was designed to face page 307 of the 1854 edition. In that context it illustrates Thoreau's search for the pond's bottom, which culminates in an important discovery:

When I had mapped the pond by the scale of ten rods to an inch, and put down the soundings, more than a hundred in all, I observed this remarkable coinci-

8

dence. Having noticed that the number indicating the greatest depth was apparently in the centre of the map, I laid a rule on the map lengthwise, and then breadthwise, and found, to my surprise, that the line of greatest length intersected *exactly* at the point of greatest depth . . . and I said to myself, Who knows but this hint would conduct to the deepest part of the ocean as well as of a pond or puddle? (*W*: ii, 309-10)

The lithograph might seem to contradict Thoreau, since on it the pond's greatest depth, 102 feet, does not appear at the intersection of base lines. The base lines, however, are not the lines of greatest length and breadth; Thoreau obtained those "by measuring into the coves." The accuracy of his survey has been confirmed with modern instruments by Edward S. Deevey, Jr., in "A Re-Examination of Thoreau's Walden," *Quarterly Review of Biology*, xvii (1942), 1-11.

Some editions of *Walden* do not retain this map, despite its obvious importance. Early readers also misunderstood its purpose; a few even thought it was included for humorous reasons. Emerson told Thoreau of a friend who admired *Walden*, "but relished it merely as a capital satire and joke, and even thought that the survey and map of the pond were not real, but a caricature of the Coast Surveys" (*J*: vii, 102-03).

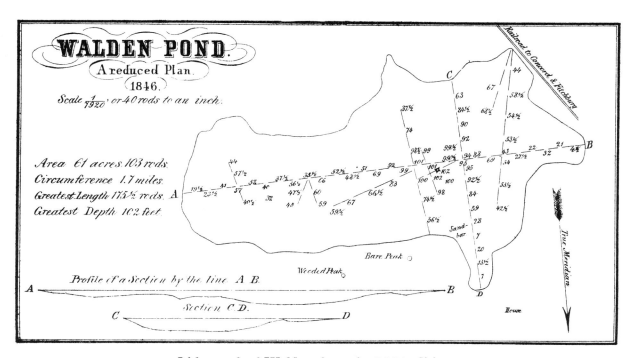

Lithograph of Walden, from the 1854 edition.

Walden

❧ MAP SIX ❧

ACTING under the authority of a town grant, H. F. Walling, a Boston surveyor, completed this map of Concord in 1852 with the aid of a local "Civ. Engʳ." named H. D. Thoreau. Walling freely adapted Thoreau's draftsmanship; a comparison of this Walden Pond with the 1846 drawing indicates considerable revision. Thoreau had calculated Walden's area at 61 acres, but Walling has 64 acres. Other notable changes are a "rounding" of the southern cove, greater extension of the southeast and southwest coves, and a radical alteration of the entire western shoreline. The reader should also note that north in this map is in the normal position, at the *top*.

The village and its surroundings appear as they were during the years Thoreau worked on the *Walden* manuscript (1849-54). Walling cites R. W. Emerson's home on both the county and village maps, either in testimony to the writer's prominence or the "middling" location of his property. Scale for the county map is 610 yards to the inch (approx. 1:22,000), and 200 yards to the inch (approx. 1:7,200) for the village map. Thoreau may have received a complimentary copy of the map for his assistance; one believed to be his survives in the Middlebury College Library. No copy is known to exist which bears his corrections of Walling's refinements.

Concord village in 1841; an engraving by J. W. Barber. Left to right:
courthouse, Unitarian church, Middlesex Hotel.

11

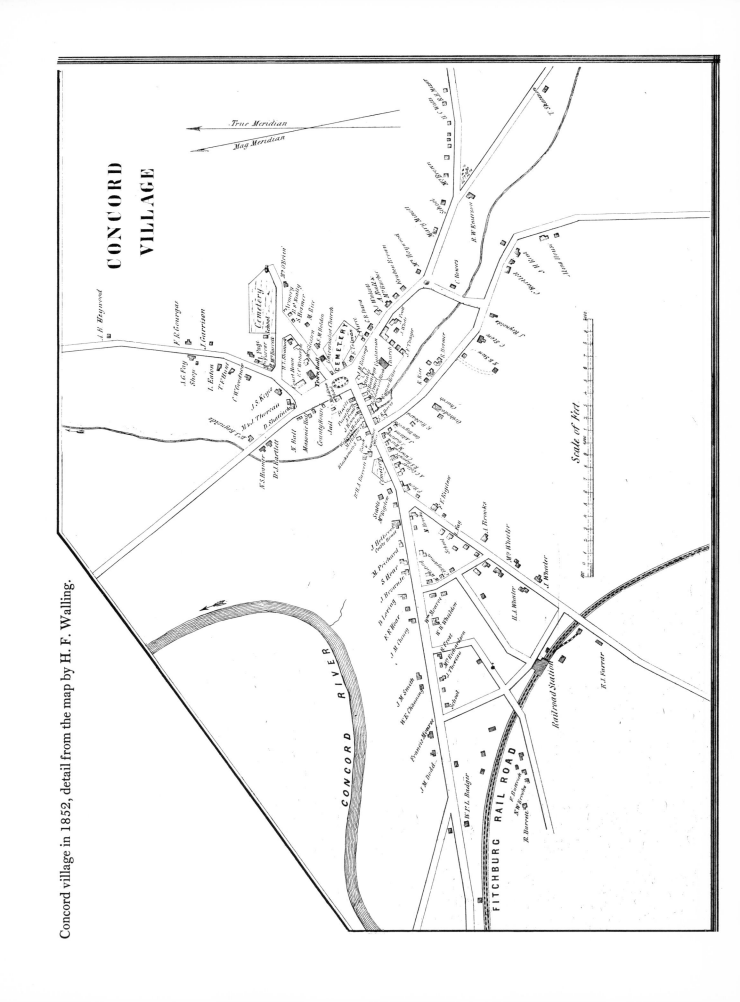

Concord village in 1852, detail from the map by H. F. Walling.

The Maine Woods

☙ MAP SEVEN ❧

THOREAU'S three journeys to the Maine interior (1846, 1853, 1857) were more than simple vacation excursions. On each trip he explored the wilderness and studied Indian culture, seeking always to clarify his ideas about America's past, present, and future. He traveled various routes by a variety of means: buggy, train, steamer, canoe, and on foot; but each time he came back convinced that his basic faith in nature was still justified. The woods were a place of "perpetual youth" and "the raw material of all our civilization"; the Indian who lived in their midst was a reminder that "intelligence flows in other channels than I knew" (*W*: III, ix, 89, 172).

This reconstruction depicts the area Thoreau covered during his three trips. In 1846 he went from Bangor to Oldtown, canoed up the Penobscot River to Sowadehunk Falls, and then hiked to the summit of Mt. Ktaadn. In 1853 he went from Bangor to Monson, crossed the length of Moosehead Lake by steamer, and then canoed up the West Branch of the Penobscot to the headwaters of Lake Chesuncook. In 1857 he followed the same route, by canoe only, and continued beyond Chesuncook through the Allegash flowage—Chamberlain Lake, Telos Lake, Webster Pond, and Grand Lake—before turning south on the Penobscot's East Branch and then returning to the main river.

Thoreau rode in a batteau of this type from Oldtown to Indian Island during his 1853 trip to Maine. Photograph by George H. Hallowell.

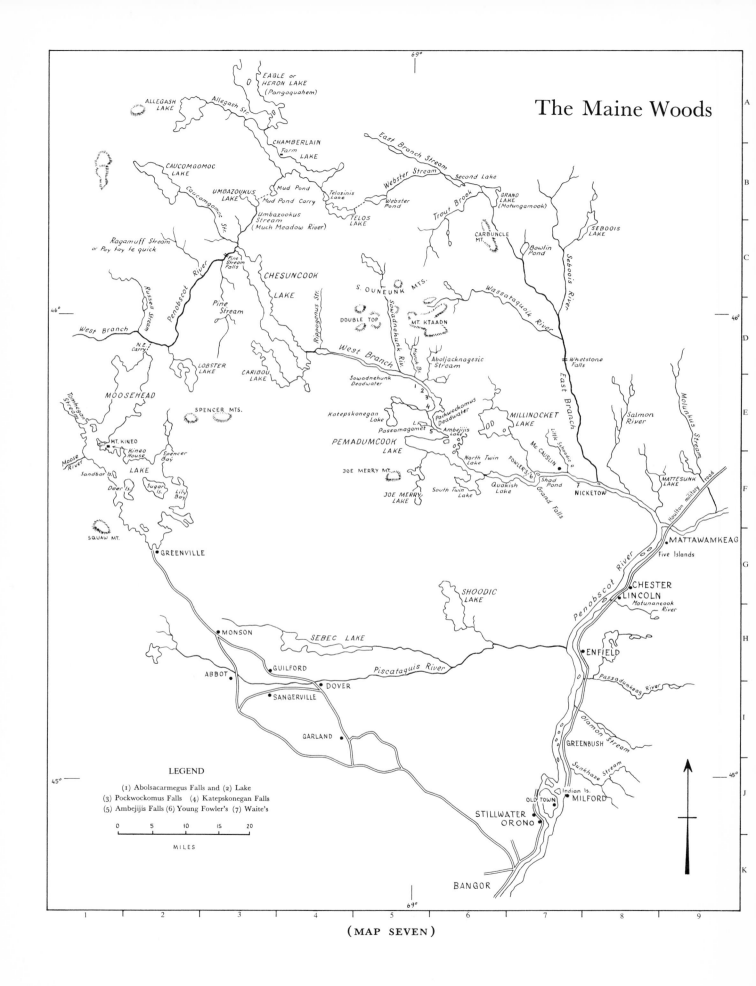

The Maine Woods

EAGLE or HERON LAKE (Pongoquahem)

ALLEGASH LAKE

Allegash Str.

CHAMBERLAIN Farm LAKE

East Branch Stream

CAUCOMGOMOC LAKE

Caucomgomoc Str.

UMBAZOUKUS LAKE

Mud Pond

Mud Pond Carry

Webster Stream

Telasinis Lake

Second Lake

GRAND LAKE (Motungamook)

Umbazookus Stream (Much Meadow River)

Webster Pond

Trout Brook

CARBUNCLE MT.

SEBOOIS LAKE

Ragamuff Stream or Pay tay te quick

TELOS LAKE

Bowlin Pond

Pine Stream Falls

Penobscot River

Russell Stream

CHESUNCOOK LAKE

Pine Stream

Ripogenus Str.

S. OUNEUNK MTS.

Wassataquoik River

Seboois River

West Branch

DOUBLE TOP

Sowadnehunk Riv.

MT. KTAADN

Whetstone Falls

N.E. Carry

LOBSTER LAKE

CARIBOU LAKE

West Branch

Sowadnehunk Deadwater

Murch Br.

Aboljacknagesic Stream

East Branch

MOOSEHEAD

Tomhegan Stream

SPENCER MTS.

1 2 3

4

Packwockomus Deadwater

MILLINOCKET LAKE

Salmon River

Molunkus Stream

Katepskonegan Lake

Passamagamet

Ambejijis Lake

Little Schoodic

Mc CAUSLIN

MT. KINEO

Kineo House

Spencer Bay

PEMADUMCOOK LAKE

North Twin Lake

FOWLER'S. 6

MATTESUNK LAKE

Moose River

Sandbar Is.

Deer Is.

Sugar Is.

Lily Bay

LAKE

JOE MERRY MT.

South Twin Lake

Quakish Lake

Grand Falls

Shad Pond

7

NICKETOW

Haulton military road

SQUAW MT.

JOE MERRY LAKE

GREENVILLE

SHOODIC LAKE

Penobscot River

MATTAWAMKEAG

Five Islands

CHESTER

LINCOLN

Matunancook River

MONSON

SEBEC LAKE

Piscataquis River

ENFIELD

Passadumkeag River

ABBOT

GUILFORD

DOVER

SANGERVILLE

GARLAND

GREENBUSH

Olamon Stream

Sunkhaze Stream

Indian Is.

OLD TOWN

MILFORD

STILLWATER

ORONO

BANGOR

LEGEND

(1) Abolsacarmegus Falls and (2) Lake
(3) Pockwockomus Falls   (4) Katepskonegan Falls
(5) Ambejijis Falls (6) Young Fowler's (7) Waite's

0   5   10   15   20

MILES

(MAP SEVEN)

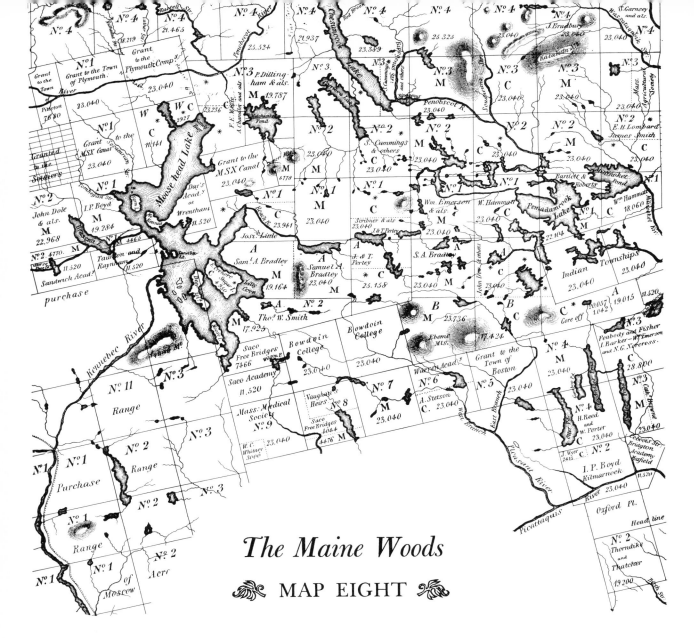

The Maine Woods

❦ MAP EIGHT ❦

ON HIS first trip to Maine (1846) Thoreau carefully traced the popular Greenleaf's *Map of Maine* only to discover later that it was "a labyrinth of errors" (*W: III, 16*). The most reliable plan of the area, he decided, was the *Map of Public Lands of Maine and Massachusetts*, a portion of which appears here. This was Thoreau's own copy, as some faint penciled notations indicate. During the two later trips he noted errors in the map and wrote in his own corrections. Unfortunately, the notes are too faint to be reproduced clearly. All of them appear in the northwest quandrant; they consist of names Thoreau supplied for previously unidentified features and his corrections of distances and areas. This is a cadastral map, meaning that it depicts the boundaries and ownership of land. Letters and numbers appearing throughout function as points of reference, but not with the consistency of a standard grid.

The Maine Woods

ON HIS second trip (1853) Thoreau had occasion to study Colton's *Map of Maine*, an enlarged section of which appears here. Although the map is not completely accurate, as Thoreau noted, it does offer a contemporary view of the area he covered during all three trips. Bangor, always his starting point, appears in the south; Mt. Ktaadn, Moosehead Lake, and Lake Chesuncook are obvious features to the north. The map's original scale was 20 miles to the inch (1:1,250,000); the area depicted is approximately 68-70° west longitude, 44° 40' - 46° 20' north latitude.

Thoreau returned from Bangor in the steamer *Boston* at the end of his 1853 trip to Maine.

16

Cape Cod

❧ MAP TEN ❧

VARIETY was the hallmark of Thoreau's four journeys to Cape Cod. In 1849 he traveled with Channing by train from Bridgewater to Sandwich, by stage to Orleans, and by foot to Provincetown. During their walk, the two men visited Eastham, Wellfleet, and Highland Light. In 1850 Thoreau returned to Provincetown, this time alone, and walked as far south as Chatham before returning for the Boston steamer. During their brief stay in 1855, Thoreau and Channing confined themselves to the northern end of the peninsula: their longest hike that year was to North Truro. Thoreau's farewell visit in 1857 was much longer and more adventurous. Solitary once again, he took a train from Plymouth to Sandwich, and then walked southeast to Harwich before turning north for a long trek to Provincetown. He "wrote up" all of these trips, the first three as *Cape Cod* (1855, 1864) and the last for his *Journal* (*J*: IX, 415-455).

On his four excursions Thoreau learned all that he could about the topography of

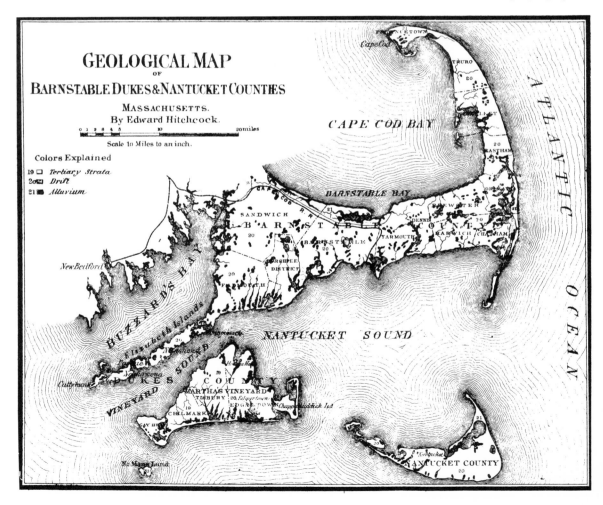

PROVINCETOWN 1858.

Cape Cod at left and Provincetown above; details from the map by H. F. Walling.

that "bare and bended arm of Massachusetts." He found that a good compass and map were his best guides, because few natives knew much about the terrain away from their regularly beaten paths. Existing maps of the Cape may also have seemed inadequate to him, for he drew his own on at least three occasions. Perhaps even they were not enough, in the face of actual experience:

> It was not as on the map, or seen from the stage coach; but there I found it all out of doors, huge and real, Cape Cod! as it cannot be represented on a map, color it as you will; the thing itself, than which there is nothing more like it, no truer picture or account; which you cannot go farther and see. (*W*: IV, 65)

This map of Cape Cod (page 20) may not be "the thing itself," but even Thoreau would have agreed that it is "huge and real." Measuring 62 by 58 inches in the original, it was designed and sold by H. F. Walling, whose firm also published the 1852 map of Concord (see Map 6). The present map is part of a series, begun in 1854, for which Walling constructed separate maps of each county in Massachusetts—thereby earning for himself the semi-official title of "Superintendent of the State Map." This map, which in its entirety depicts the counties of Barnstable, Dukes, and Nantucket, is an excellent example of Walling's detailed cartography. Drawn at a scale of one mile to an inch (1:63,360), the map includes a wealth of natural and artificial features. Because its date almost coincides with that of Thoreau's last visit, the map offers us a convenient guide to the Cape Cod that he knew so well.

(MAP TEN)

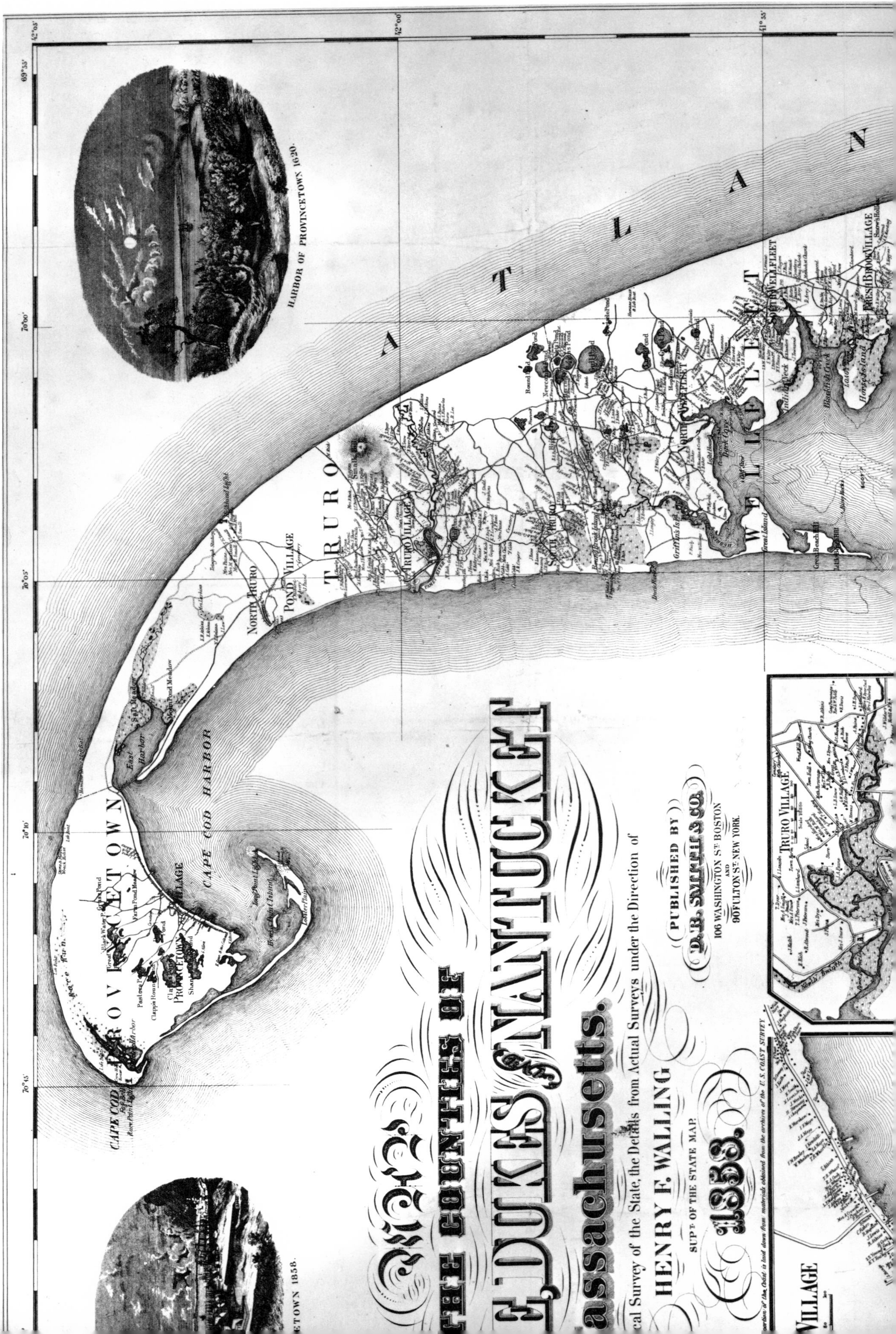

HARBOR OF PROVINCETOWN 1620.

A T L A N T

TRURO

WELLFLEET

NORTH TRURO

POND VILLAGE

PROVINCETOWN

CAPE COD HARBOR

Cape Cod Harbor

East Harbor

Sag Marsh

Long Point Light

Race Point Light

CAPE COD

COUNTIES OF
DUKES & NANTUCKET
Massachusetts.

Topographical Survey of the State, the Details from Actual Surveys under the Direction of
HENRY F. WALLING
SUP.T OF THE STATE MAP
1858.

(PUBLISHED BY)
D. R. SMITH & CO.
106 WASHINGTON ST. BOSTON
AND
90 FULTON ST. NEW YORK.

TRURO VILLAGE

PROVINCETOWN 1858.

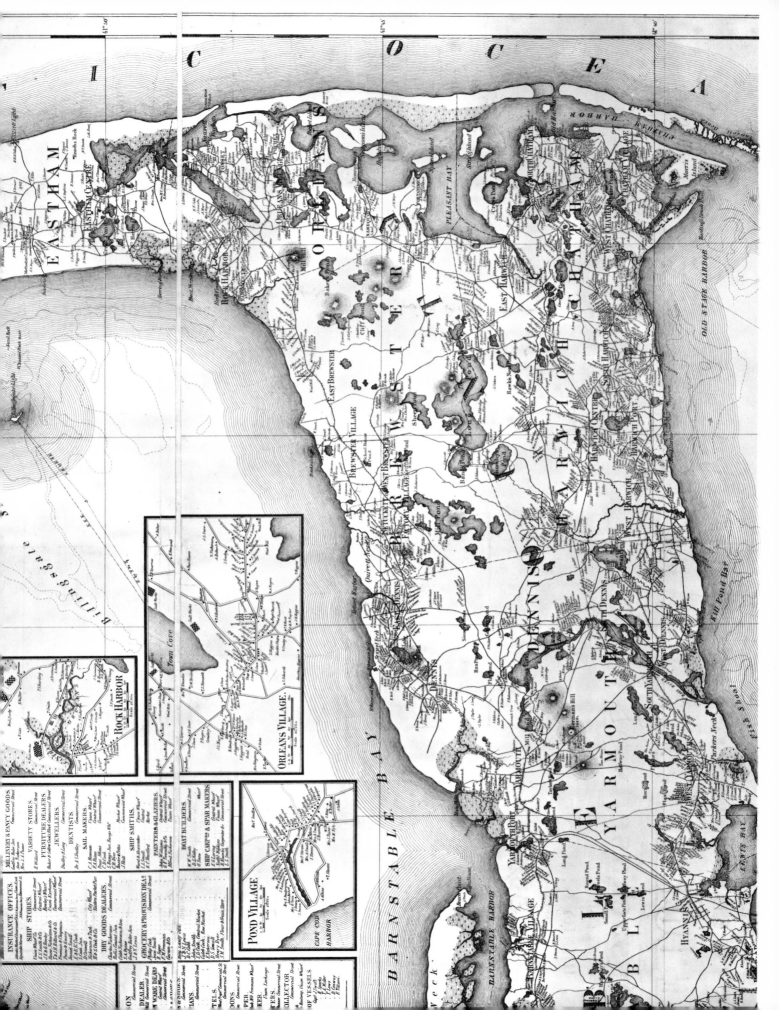

70°10'

Race Pt. Lt
Watches Hbr
Pt P
CAPTE
Sand R
House Pt
Long Pt Lt
Pond vil
Highland Lt 1798

Small Hill
Pond R

Bound Brook Isl
Herring R
Gull
Duck Har. Griffins
Long P
North Vil.
Duck Cr
Great I
Pleas. Valley vil
Lombard's pt
Beach I
Wellfleet Bay
Blackfish Cr.
South Vil.

Horse or Lieut.
Brook vil.

Billingsgate I
Sloop Spring
Bill Lt
Cook's Brook
Br R
Pd.
pretty good for corn
Nausett Lt.

200 a good land or any to corn'd
with 3 cedar swamps on

41°50'

Snow Brook
Grape
Pilg. land d
4m.
Great P
200
Herring P
Great mead R?
Boat mead R
M
Herring
Nausett Har.
Bank R
Souket Cr
Roads

Breakwater
Mill Hill
mid Pochia I

Her.
Sursute
Quivet Ct
Pastor vil
Sheep P
Filon
N. Dennis
Scargo H.
Packt Sig.
Hill
N. Boston R
Garry P
Bangs P
Long P.
Hinckley
Roads
Pleasant Bay

Bass Hole
Pleasant
Sandy neck
Beach Pt L
Run P
Herring R
Muddy Cr
Chat. sta.
Har.
Billings P
Raads
J
Roads
Yarmouth Port
Kelleys Bay
German's H.
△ 138
S. Harwich vil.
Oyster
Chatham Hbr
Nausett Beach
Swan
Oyster Har
Harding's Beach
41°40'
Hyannis
Bass P
Cranvill Vil. Keeleys P
Swan P
Stage Har.
Lewis Bay
Hyannis Har
Pt. Gammon Lt
Wreck Cove

N

1 2 3 4 5 6 7 8 9 10 11 12 13 14 15
Monomoy
Bishops Clerks
Powder hole

Cape Cod
❧ MAP ELEVEN ❧

THIS general view of the cape, from Hyannis to Race Point, is either a tracing or a copy Thoreau made from a contemporary source—possibly the "Gazetteer" he carried during his early visits. He apparently omitted some of the details on the original map, especially "Roads" in the southeast that he avoided while hiking. Some of the noted features refer to personal experiences: "200 [acres] good land as any in Concord" and "pretty good for corn," for example, point to the coastal walk of 1850. Most of the symbols—dots for houses, triangles for hills, and ♂ for churches—probably appeared on the original map. The legend "Bishops Clerks" (lower left) refers to obstructions in Nantucket Sound.

"Beach Bluffs, Wellfleet Shore." Photograph by Herbert W. Gleason.

23

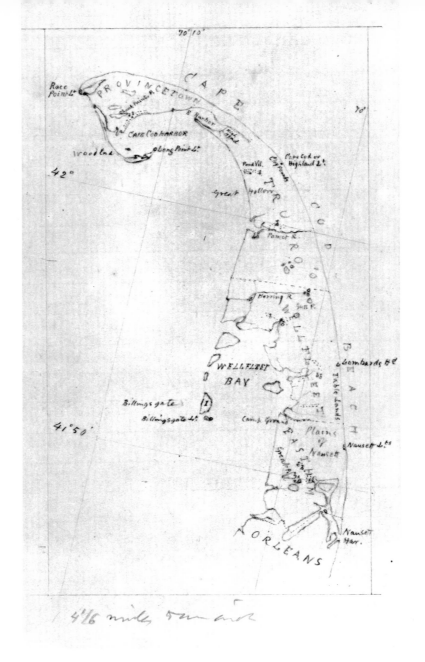

❧ MAP TWELVE ❧

THIS MAP, an original drawing by Thoreau, depicts the portion of Cape Cod that he knew best. He walked the full distance between Orleans and Provincetown during three of his journeys, and he spent most of his brief stay in 1850 at Highland Light. The map's precision reflects his familiarity with the area; several of the details—[Eastham] "Camp Ground," "Plains of Nauset," "Great Hollow"—are personal additions. He has carefully drawn the projection, the township names, and the symbols for hills and churches. For some reason, possibly because of space limitations, he tilted the drawing away from a normal perpendicular.

Cape Cod

❧ MAP THIRTEEN ❧

THE final map of Cape Cod, also an original drawing, is Thoreau's most sophisticated piece of cartography. No place names appear, but the region is obviously the same as that of the preceding map. The scale is much larger here, however; and this difference accounts for the greater degree of physical detail in features like Nauset Harbor, Wellfleet Bay, and Palmer River. The radials emanating from the drawing's center resemble a lighthouse, but they are only Thoreau's device for maintaining proportion in his draft.

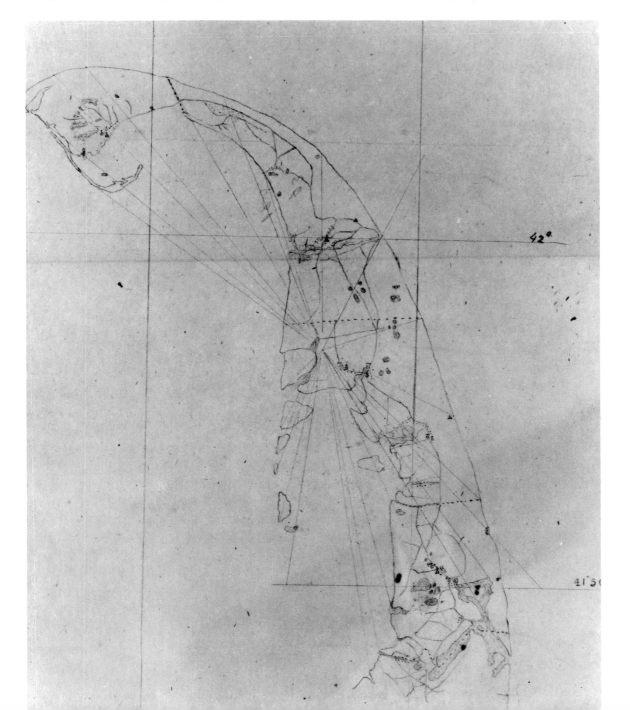

Thoreau returned from Provincetown to Boston in 1849 on the steamer *Naushon*.

A Yankee in Canada

 MAP FOURTEEN

THOREAU'S trip to Canada in 1850 was a disappointing venture, mostly because he was not able to study the terrain carefully in advance. Maps were a particular problem; adequate ones were just not available in Concord at the time. As compensation he copied Canadian maps while on the trip and asked natives to suggest additional details. After his return, he read a number of books on Canada and studied supplementary maps at the Harvard Library. From this research he eventually produced a lecture, a full-length manuscript (pub. 1866), a voluminous notebook, and at least two original maps.

This reconstruction offers a pictorial guide to Thoreau's Canadian journey. He and Ellery Channing traveled by rail from Boston to Burlington, Vermont, and then took a steamer across Lake Champlain to Plattsburg, New York. Most accounts have the two men proceeding north to St. John by train, but in all likelihood they took another steamer. The railroad between Plattsburg and Montreal was still under construction in 1850; service from Rouse's Point to St. John did not exist until 1851. Thoreau and Channing therefore had to book steamer passage at least to St. John; from there a train did run to Montreal. The map's Legend identifies points of interest that the two men visited in the vicinities of Montreal and Quebec.

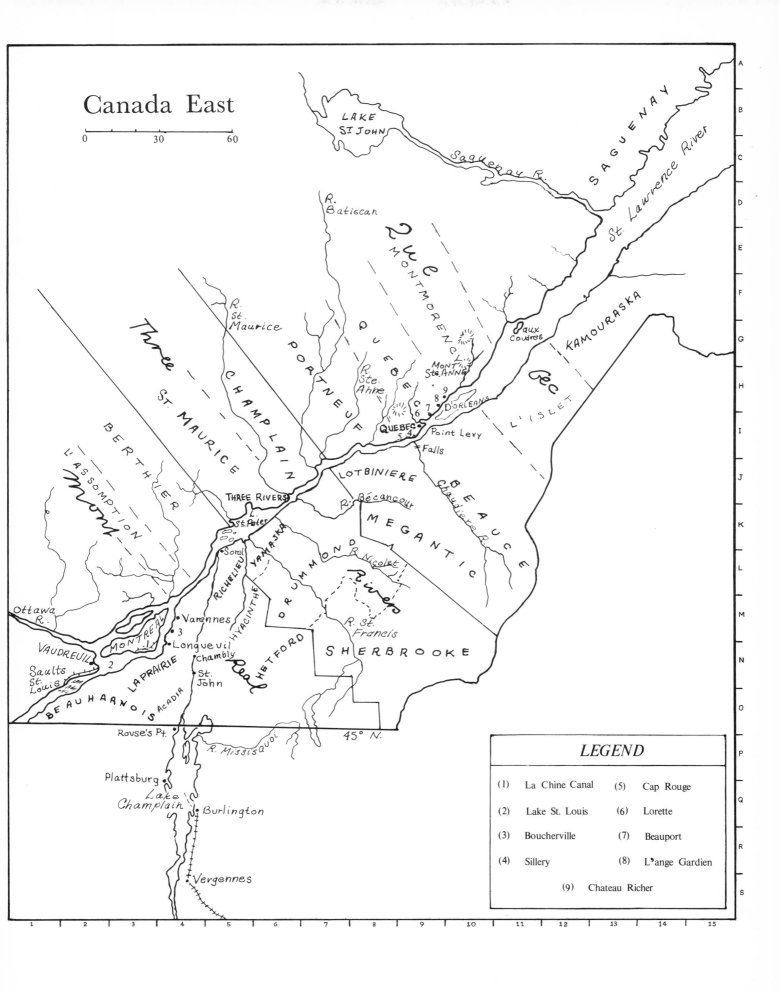

Canada East

0   30   60

LAKE ST JOHN

SAGUENAY R.

SAGUENAY

St. Lawrence River

R. Batiscan

Q u e
MONTMORENCY

R. St. Maurice

PORTNEUF

CHAMPLAIN

Three

ST. MAURICE

R. Ste. Ahne

R. Ste. Anne

QUEBEC

MONT. Ste. ANNE

aux Coudres

KAMOURASKA

L'ISLET

bec

BEAUCE

Chaudiere R.

D'ORLEANS

8 9
6 7

QUEBEC
5 4

Point Levy

Falls

BERTHER

L'ASSOMPTION

THREE RIVERS

L. St. Peter

LOTBINIERE

R. Bécancour

MEGANTIC

R. Nicolet

Sorel

RICHELIEU

YAMASKA

DRUMMOND

River

R. St. Francis

SHERBROOKE

Ottawa R.

MONTREAL I.

Varennes

3

Longueuil

Chambly

HYACINTHE

VAUDREUIL

2

LA PRAIRIE

ACADIA

St. John

HETFORD

Saults St. Louis

BEAUHARNOIS

Rouse's Pt.

45° N.

R. Missisquoi

Plattsburg

Lake Champlain

Burlington

Vergennes

LEGEND

(1)	La Chine Canal	(5)	Cap Rouge
(2)	Lake St. Louis	(6)	Lorette
(3)	Boucherville	(7)	Beauport
(4)	Sillery	(8)	L'ange Gardien
		(9)	Chateau Richer

A Yankee in Canada

❧ MAP FIFTEEN ❧

ON HIS last day in Quebec, Thoreau found himself with some time to spare:

> . . . remembering that large map of Canada which I had seen in the parlor of the restaurant in my search after pudding, and realizing that I might never see the like out of the country, I returned thither, asked liberty to look at the map, rolled up the mahogany table, put my handkerchief on it, stood on it, and copied all I

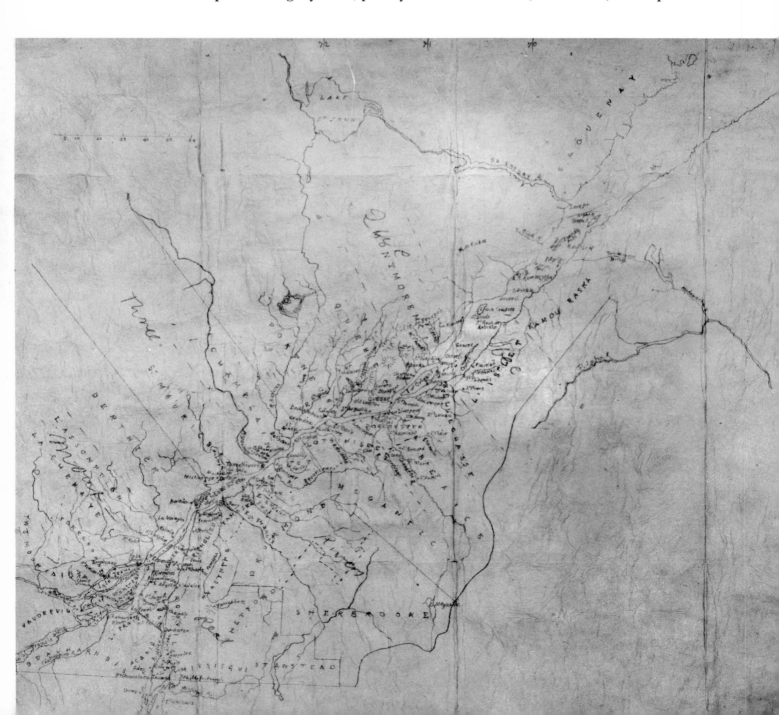

View of Quebec in 1850; a drawing by Captain B. Beaufoy.

wanted before the maid came in and said to me standing on the table, "Some gentlemen want the room, sir;" and I retreated without having broken the neck of a single bottle, or my own, very thankful and willing to pay for all the solid food I had got. (*W*: v, 95)

This map may possibly be the same one, but it certainly contains more detail than Thoreau could have copied in a short while. In all likelihood, he added most of the place names during his later studies. The map he copied was apparently the western portion of "Nelson's New Map of British Provinces in North America" (1840). Thoreau's copy and the Nelson map have identical lettering and scales, but Thoreau has omitted some towns and added symbols for mountains.

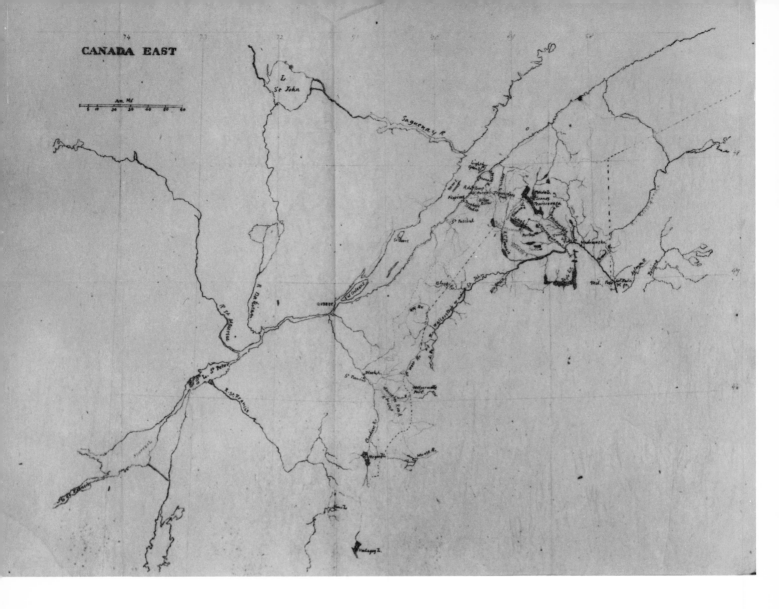

✤ MAP SIXTEEN ✤

AN ORIGINAL tracing by Thoreau, this map covers the same general area as its predecessor, but with less detail and on a reduced scale. Whereas the previous map concentrates on the shores and tributaries of the St. Lawrence River, this one features an area south of the Gaspé peninsula and some river systems in western Maine. Thoreau probably drew this map in connection with his later Indian studies (1853-60), for he noted more natural features—bearing Indian names—than French villages. His eleven notebook volumes on the Indian contain several tracings, similar to this one, of early American maps; and his Canadian notebook has a large section devoted to the early cartography of Canada and the Eastern United States. The latter volume is fully described in Lawrence Willson's article, "Thoreau's Canadian Notebook," *Huntington Library Quarterly*, XXII (1959), 179-200.

A Yankee in Canada

❧ MAP SEVENTEEN ❧

THIS MAP is from a larger plan of the city of Quebec that is contemporaneous (1851) with Thoreau's visit. During the tour he viewed the usual attractions, including the city's fortifications and gardens, neither of which impressed him favorably:

> Huge stone structures of all kinds, both in their erection and by their influence when erected, rather oppress than liberate the mind. They are tombs for the souls of men, as frequently for their bodies also. (*W*: v, 78)

On his first walk around the Upper Town, Thoreau started at the Castle Garden, continued through the suburbs to the King's Woodyard (Government Fuel Yard); then returned by way of Mountain Street and Prescott Gate.

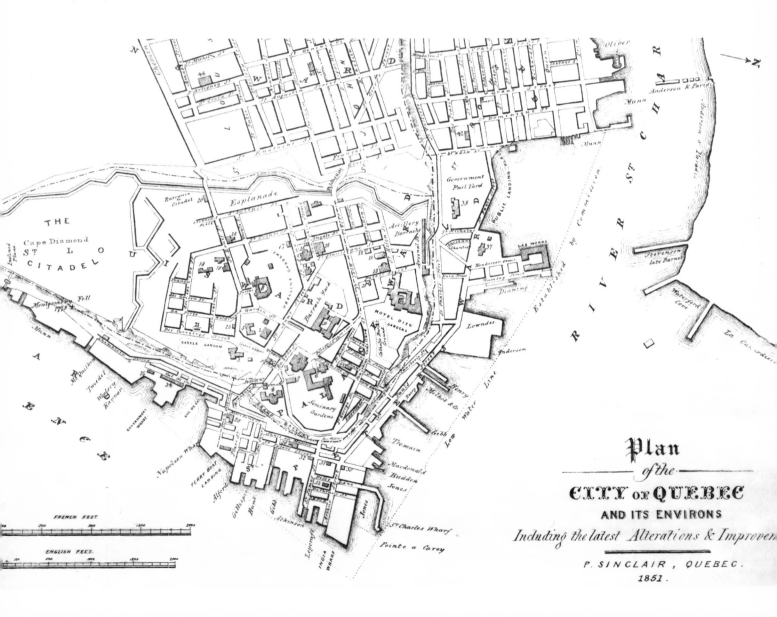

Plan
of the
CITY OF QUEBEC
AND ITS ENVIRONS
Including the latest Alterations & Improven

P. SINCLAIR, QUEBEC.
1851.

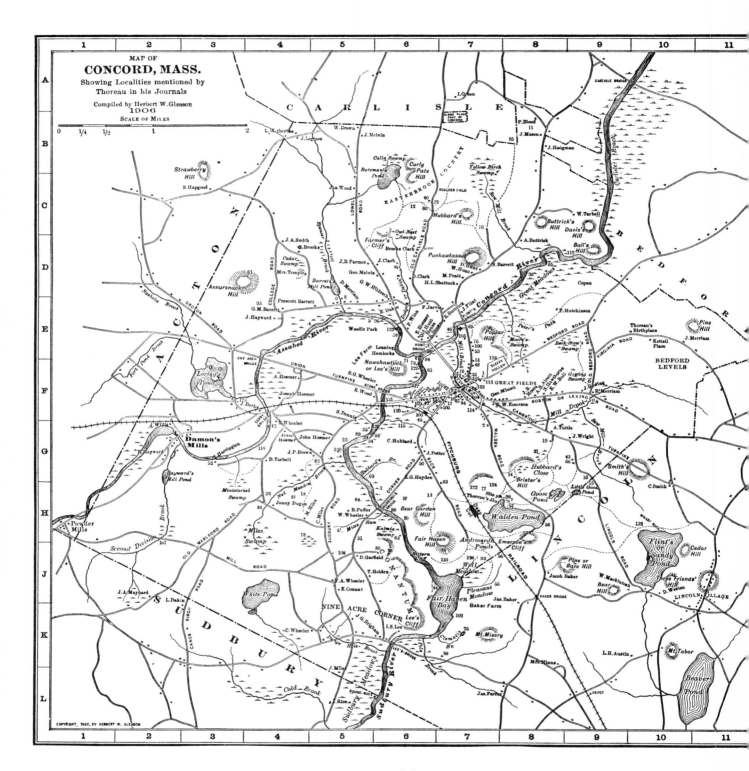

MAP OF
CONCORD, MASS.

Showing Localities mentioned by
Thoreau in his Journals

Compiled by Herbert W. Gleason
1906
SCALE OF MILES

COPYRIGHT, 1907, BY HERBERT W. GLEASON

32

The Journal

✵ MAP EIGHTEEN ✵
Concord

HERBERT W. GLEASON (1855-1937), a photographer and naturalist from Boston, drew this map for the 1906 edition of Thoreau's complete *Writings*. He used Thoreau's drawings whenever possible, interviewed older residents, and relied heavily upon his personal knowledge of the area. His photographs of local scenery also appeared in the edition; today they are still among the finest ever taken of the "Concord Country." Gleason's map is loyal to Thoreau's unconventional place names and for all its detail, it is a highly accurate depiction. Two errors were noted, however, by Mrs. Caleb Wheeler in the April, 1945 issue of the *Thoreau Society Bulletin*: Davis' Hill (C-9) should be on the other side of the river, and Kettel Place (E-10) should be opposite Emerson's House (F-7), not Thoreau's Birthplace.

Note to Map of Concord

BY H. W. GLEASON

"The material used in this Map of Concord has been derived from a variety of sources. The town bounds, streets, and residences have been taken from a township map of Middlesex County made by H. F. Walling in 1856, reference also being had to a local map of Concord by the same engineer, dated 1852, on which credit for the surveys of White Pond and Walden Pond is given to 'H. D. Thoreau, Civ. Eng^r.' The course of the Concord River is drawn from an elaborate manuscript plan of Thoreau's, based on earlier surveys, showing the river from East Sudbury to Billerica Dam. This plan, on which Thoreau has entered the results of his investigation of the river in the summer of 1859, is now in the Concord Public Library. The outlines of Walden and White Ponds have also been taken from Thoreau's original surveys, now in the Concord Library. Loring's and Bateman's Ponds are according to surveys by Mr. Albert E. Wood of Concord, and Flint's Pond is from a survey for the Concord Water Works by Mr. William Wheeler, also of Concord.

"All names of places are those used by Thoreau, no attention being given to other names perhaps more current either in his own time or at present. Only such names of residents are given as are mentioned in the Journal.

"A few old wood roads, pasture lanes, etc. (Thoreau's preferred highways), are indicated, as to their general direction, by dotted lines.

"The irregularity of the northeastern boundary of Concord arose from the fact that when Carlisle was set off from Concord in 1780, the farmers living on the border were given the option of remaining within the bounds of Concord or of being included in the new town. In 1903 the Massachusetts Legislature abolished this old division and continued the straight line forming the western half of the boundary directly to the river.

"The identification of localities which were named by Thoreau apparently for his personal use alone has been accomplished, so far as it has proceeded, by a careful study of all the Journal references to each locality, an examination of a large number of Thoreau's manuscript surveys, and an extended personal investigation on the ground. Many of these localities are given more than one name in the Journal, and in a few cases the same name is given to different localities. Where doubt exists as to any particular location, the name is omitted from the map.

"Hon. F. B. Sanborn, Judge John S. Keyes, Dr. Edward W. Emerson, the Misses Hosmer, and other among the older residents of Concord have been consulted in the preparation of the map, and have kindly supplied helpful information from their personal acquaintance with Thoreau."

December, 1906

"Leaning Hemlocks" on the Assabet River (E-6). Photograph by Herbert W. Gleason.

Above: View from Fairhaven Hill (H-7), looking north to Concord.

Below: Hunt's Bridge on the Concord River (E-6), looking north up the Lowell Road.

Photographs by Herbert W. Gleason.

Hubbard's Bridge on the Concord River (H-6). Photograph by Herbert W. Gleason.

The Journal

 MAP NINETEEN
Concord

BY PRESENTING Concord's topography in relief, this map complements the Gleason survey of 1906. The relief map is a compromise between Walling's map (1852), a reconnaissance survey (1886), and the topographic sheets of the U. S. Geological Survey (1950, 1958). A comparison of all four maps indicates that several changes have occurred in the area's physical features since Thoreau's day—most notably, in the various bodies of water. Thoreau, of course, anticipated some of these changes as a consequence of his limnological studies. Topographical relief is the map's most important feature; the few roads appearing on it serve only as points of reference.

36

71° 20'

71° 22' 30"

71° 25'

Ball's Hill

Smith's Hill

Lincoln

Flint's Pond

Virginia Rd.

Lincoln Road

Pine Hill

Goose Pond

Brister's Hill

Beck Stow's Swamp

Bedford Road

Lexington Road

Walden Rd.

Walden Pond

Mill Brook

CONCORD

Thoreau's Cabin

Baker Farm

CONCORD RIVER

Great Meadows

Ponkatawset Hill

N. Bridge

Back Rd.

Fairhaven Hill

Fair Haven Bay

Old Carlisle Rd.

Dakin's Br.

Nawshawtuct Hill

Bear Garden Hill

CONANTUM

Lee's Cliff

Lowell Rd.

Conner Rd.

Sudbury River

Spencer Brook

Lee Farm

Assabet River

Kalmia Swamp

Sudbury Road

Nine Acre Corner

Nut Meadow Brook

Miles Swamp

White Pond

Annursnack Hill

Fitchburg Railroad

Hayward's Mill Pond

Powder Mill Road

Nashoba Brook

Union Turnpike

N

SCALE 1:24 000

CONTOUR INTERVAL 10 FEET

DATUM IS MEAN SEA LEVEL

½ MILE

1 MILE

(MAP NINETEEN)

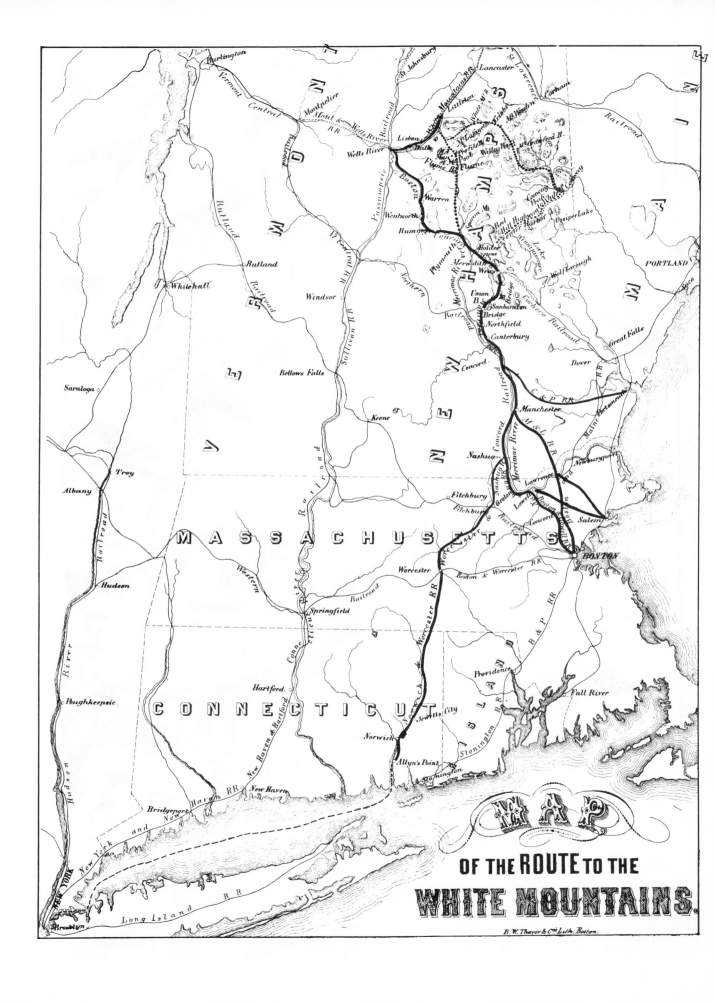

MAP

OF THE ROUTE TO THE

WHITE MOUNTAINS.

B. W. Thayer & Cⁿ Lith. Boston.

The Journal

❧ MAP TWENTY ❧
The White Mountains

THOREAU'S major excursion for the summer of 1858 was to the same area he had visited nearly twenty years earlier with his brother John. His companion this time was Edward Hoar, a young student who shared Thoreau's interest in "botanizing" and therefore traveled frequently with him in the later years.

Journeying by hired horse and wagon, the men left Concord on July 2 and reached Center Harbor, New Hampshire in two days. They spent the next several days climbing Red Hill, Mt. Chocorua, and Mt. Washington. At the summit of Mt. Washington Thoreau discovered that a map he had copied was inaccurate, so he guided the party by compass reckoning to Tuckerman's Ravine. They remained in that area another day or so, and then traveled north to Franconia Notch. On July 15 they turned south again, and four days later they were back in Concord.

Thoreau enjoyed the trip, even though he was constantly plagued by ill fortune. Heavy fogs and rains often obscured the scenery; campfires went out of control twice, the second time causing considerable forest damage; he tore his nails while climbing and then severely sprained an ankle. Still, he had seen fresh scenery and collected new botanical data, so the whole trip provided, as he later wrote in the *Journal* account, "relief and expansion of my thoughts" (*J*: xi, 4).

This map depicts the routes of various commercial excursions to the White Mountains. Although Thoreau and Hoar traveled privately, they followed closely the route outlined here from Lowell, Massachusetts to Holderness, New Hampshire. References in the text to an unopened "White Mountains Railroad" indicate that the map was printed shortly before Thoreau's visit. The copy printed here, in fact, is believed to be Thoreau's own.

Rearranged detail from the White Mountains map.

Above: Dubuque in 1858. Engraved by J. Cameron after a drawing by L. Farnham.

Below: The steamer *Itasca*, ca. 1860.

The Minnesota Journey

❧ MAP TWENTY-ONE ❧

THIS reconstruction traces the route of Thoreau's last journey (May 11-July 9, 1861), the only one he ever made into the American interior. Accompanied by Horace Mann, Jr., he traveled westward by rail, stopping a few days at Niagara Falls and Chicago before moving on to the Mississippi River at Dunleith (now East Dubuque), Illinois. There the two men boarded the steamer *Itasca* for a trip up river to St. Paul, where they arrived on May 26. On June 17 they embarked from St. Paul on the steamer *Frank Steele* for a trip up the Minnesota River to the Lower Sioux Agency near Redwood.

Returning to St. Paul on June 22, Thoreau and Mann started downstream the following day, stopped at Red Wing for four days, then continued to Prairie du Chien on the steamer *War Eagle*. They crossed Wisconsin by train; Lakes Michigan and Huron by steamers; and Ontario, New York, Vermont, and New Hampshire by train. Thoreau wrote no book about this journey; his failing health would not even permit a full account for the *Journal*. Instead, he left behind a batch of "field notes" which Walter Harding edited as *Thoreau's Minnesota Journey: Two Documents* (Geneseo, New York, 1962).

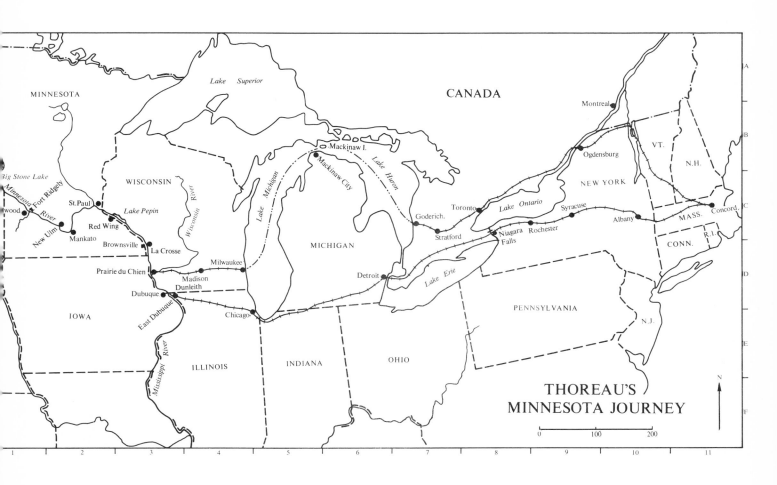

THOREAU'S
MINNESOTA JOURNEY

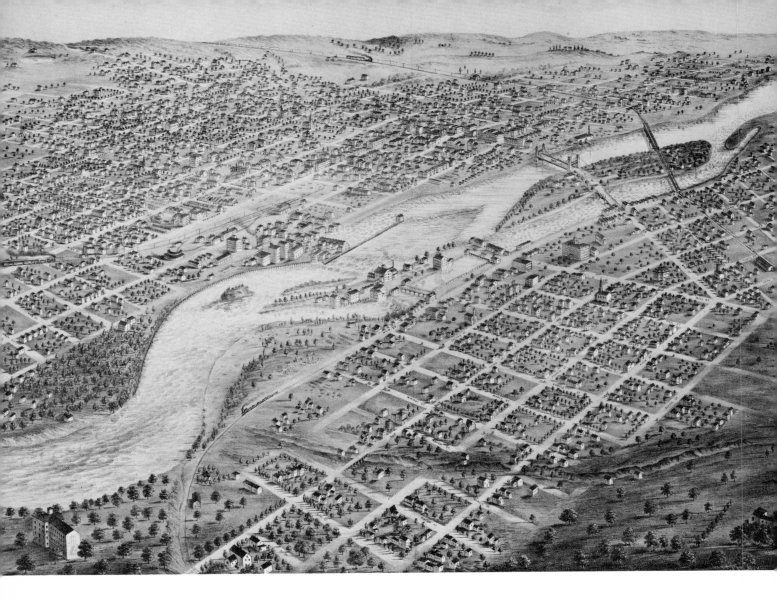

Above: View of Minneapolis, a few years after Thoreau's visit. *Below:* St. Paul in 1856.

The Minnesota Journey

❧ MAP TWENTY-TWO ❧

DURING their nine days at St. Paul, Thoreau and Mann "botanized" in the surrounding area, visiting Nicollet Island, Lake Calhoun, Minnehaha Falls, Hennepin Island, and the Mississippi River banks. On June 5 they moved to a rural boarding house situated between Lake Calhoun and Lake Harriett, where they stayed until departing for the trip to Redwood. This detail is from a late nineteenth-century map of Minneapolis and St. Paul, published by Rand, McNally and Company.

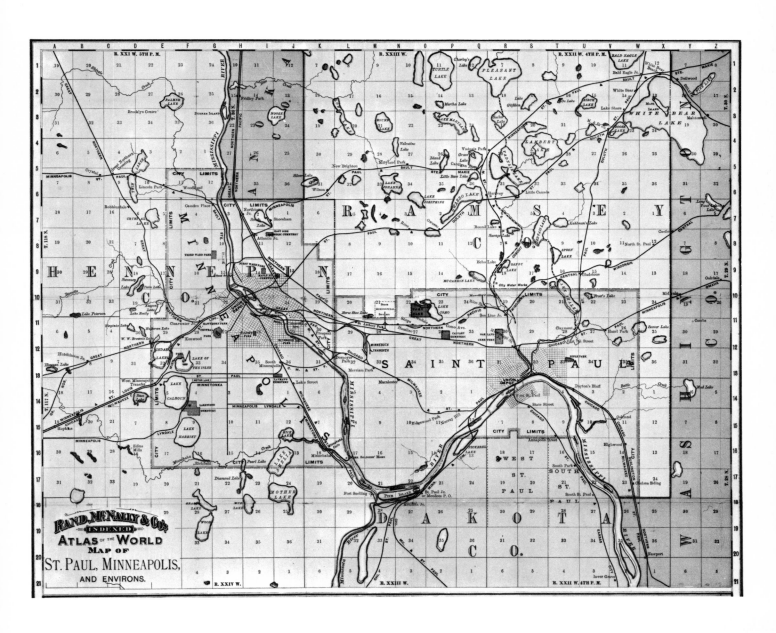

The St. Paul levee in 1859.   Thoreau traveled to Redwood on the steamer *Frank Steele* (2nd from left).

The Minnesota Journey

 MAP TWENTY-THREE

THIS MAP of Minnesota, dated 1855, depicts the territory Thoreau visited during his trip up the Minnesota River to the Lower Sioux Agency near Redwood. The map indicates the unsettled nature of the frontier at that time; its wildness suggests how Thoreau's already poor health must have been affected by primitive traveling conditions. Thoreau might well have used this map, a product of Colton and Company, even though he had previously criticized their map of Maine (see Map 9).

44

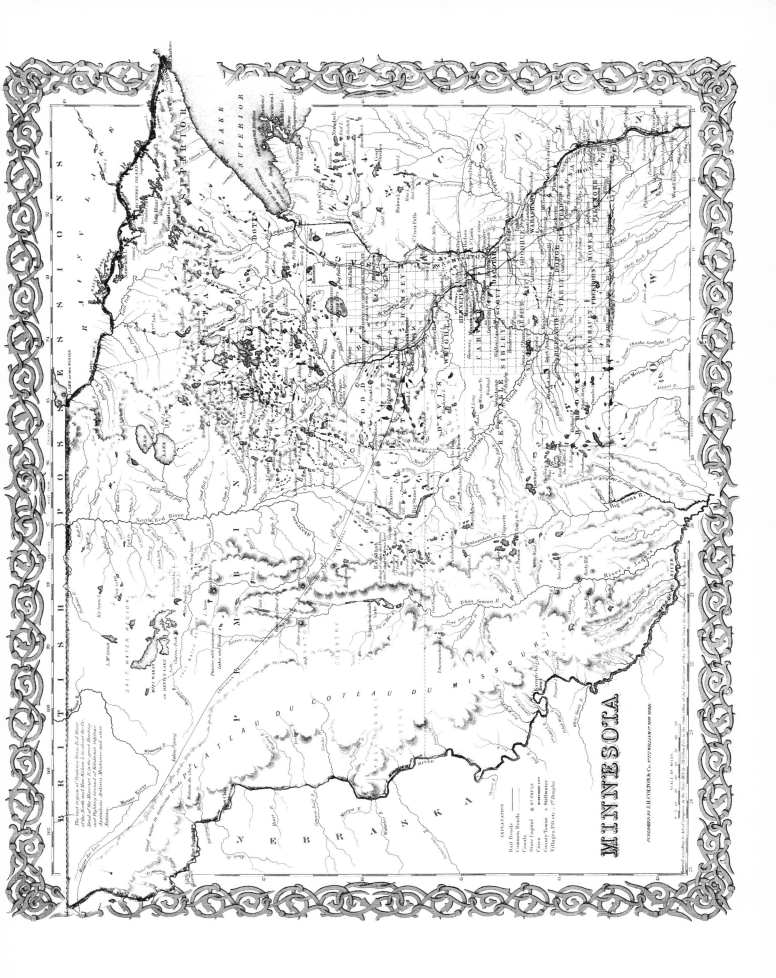

MINNESOTA

EXPLANATION
Rail Roads
Common Roads
Canals
State Capital   ⊕ ST PAULS
Cities   ⊛ HASTINGS CITY
County Towns   ⊛ Stillwater
Villages P.O. etc.   ◦ P¹ Douglas

PUBLISHED BY J. H. COLTON & Co. N.º 172 WILLIAM S.º NEW YORK.

SCALE OF MILES

Entered according to Act of Congress in the Year 1855 by J.H. Colton & Co. in the Clerks office of the District Court of the United States for the Southern District of New York

Notes on the Maps

THOREAU'S TRAVELS

MAP 1. A reconstruction, based on Henry S. Tanner, *New Hampshire and Vermont* (Philadelphia, 1833) and Dearborn's *New Map of Massachusetts* (Boston, 1848).

A WEEK ON THE CONCORD AND MERRIMACK RIVERS

MAP. 2. Thoreau's original manuscript is now in the Clifton Waller Barrett Library of American Literature, Alderman Library, University of Virginia. The map is published here by permission of Mr. Barrett and Miss Anne Freudenberg, Curator of Manuscripts at the Alderman Library.

MAP 3. Sources for the reconstruction include: Phillip Carrigan, *Map of the State of New Hampshire* (Concord, N. H., 1816); John Farmer and Jacob B. Moore, *A Gazetteer of the State of New Hampshire* (Concord, N. H., 1823); Nathan Hale, *Map of New England* (Boston, 1826); John Hayward, *The New England Gazetteer* (Boston, 1839); Eliphalet and Phineas Merrill, *A Gazetteer of the State of New Hampshire* (Exeter, N. H., 1817); J. W. Meader, *The Merrimack River* (Boston, 1869); plus topographic sheets for Massachusetts and New Hampshire from the U. S. Geological Survey.

WALDEN

MAP 4. The original manuscript is part of the Thoreau Collection at the Concord Free Public Library; it is published here by permission of the Trustees.

MAP 5. Thoreau's original drawing was given by his sister Sophia to Miss E. J. Weir of Concord; it is now in the Berg Collection of the New York Public Library. Information on the drawing was supplied by Mrs. Lola L. Szladits, Curator of the Berg Collection; permission to publish was granted by Mr. John Miller, Executive Assistant of the Library. The original lithographic stone has not survived, but the earliest print is with the page proofs of *Walden* in the Henry E. Huntington Library and Art Gallery, San Marino, California.

MAP 6. The copy believed to be Thoreau's is in the Abernethy Collection of American Literature at the Library of Middlebury College, Middlebury, Vermont. Information on that copy was provided by Mr. John R. McKenna, Librarian. The copy reprinted here was supplied by the Map and Geography Division, Library of Congress.

THE MAINE WOODS

MAP 7. The rivers and lakes in this reconstruction appear as they were in the 1850's, before logging activities and dam construction permanently altered the Maine interior. Sources include: *Colton's Railroad Map of the State of Maine* (New York, 1855); F. H. Eckstrom, "Thoreau's 'Maine Woods,'" *Atlantic Monthly* CII (July, 1908), 245-50; L. L. Hubbard, *Map of Moosehead Lake and Northern Maine* (Cambridge, Mass., 1883); and surveys by M. M. Tidd (Jamaica Plain, Mass., 1884).

MAP 8. Thoreau's personal copy is in the Thoreau Collection at the Concord Free Public Library; it is reprinted here by permission of the Trustees. Information on the penciled notations was supplied by Mrs. Marcia E. Moss, Reference Librarian.

MAP 9. This copy was supplied by the Firestone Library of Princeton University, with the assistance of Mr. Lawrence E. Spellman, Curator of Maps.

CAPE COD

MAP 10. Information on this map was supplied by Mr. Walter W. Ristow, Chief of the Geography and Map Division, Library of Congress. His article, "Nineteenth-Century Cadastral Maps in Ohio," *Papers of the Bibliographical Society of America*, LIX (1965), 306-15, contains an excellent summary of the professional career of Henry F. Walling. This copy and permission to reprint were also supplied by Mr. Ristow.

MAP 11. The original manuscript is part of the Thoreau Collection at the Concord Free Public Library; this reproduction is published by permission of the Trustees.

MAPS 12-13. Thoreau's original manuscripts are in the collection of the Henry E. Huntington Library and Art Gallery, San Marino, California; they are published here by permission of the Trustees and Dr. James E. Thorpe, Director.

A YANKEE IN CANADA

MAP 14. Information on Thoreau's mode of travel was obtained with the generous assistance of Charles T. Morrissey, Director of the Vermont Historical Society; Paul Z. Dubois, Librarian of the New York State Historical Association; John Buechler and T. D. Seymour Basset, both of the Bailey Library, University of Vermont.

MAPS 15-16. The original manuscripts are in the Thoreau Collection at the Concord Free Public Library; they are published here by permission of the Trustees. The Indian and Canadian notebooks are in the collection of the J. Pierpont Morgan Library, New York City.

MAP 17. This copy was supplied by the Map and Geography Division, Library of Congress, Washington, D. C.

47

THE JOURNAL

MAP 18. Herbert Gleason's map and explanatory note are reprinted by permission of the Houghton Mifflin Company, publisher of *The Complete Writings of Henry David Thoreau* (Boston, 1906).

MAP 19. Particular thanks are due to Theo Baumann of the Geography Department, University of Canterbury, for his work on the relief map of Concord.

MAP 20. Thoreau's copy is from the Thoreau Collection at the Concord Free Public Library; it is published here by permission of the Trustees.

THE MINNESOTA JOURNEY

MAP 21. Sources for this reconstruction include: John T. Flanagan, "Thoreau in Minnesota," *Minnesota History* XVI (March, 1935); Robert Straker, "Thoreau's Journey to Minnesota," *New England Quarterly* XIV (September, 1941), and E. B. Swanson, "The Manuscript Journal of Thoreau's Last Journey," *Minnesota History* XX (June, 1939).

MAP 22. This map was supplied by the Map and Geography Division, Library of Congress, Washington, D.C.

MAP 23. This copy was supplied by the Geography Department, University of Minnesota, with the assistance of Mr. Richard E. Sykes.

View from Nawshawtuc Hill (F-6), looking south up the Concord River.

Photograph by Herbert W. Gleason.

A Chronology of Thoreau's Travels[*]

1836	January and February	Canton, Mass.; teaches school and lives with Rev. Orestes A. Brownson (pp. 45-46).
1836	Summer	New York City with his father; family pencil business (p. 45).
1839	May	Boston to Portland, Maine, by boat; to Bath, Brunswick, Augusta, Gardiner, Oldtown, Belfast, Castine, Thomaston, and Bangor in search of a teaching job (pp. 58-59).
1839	August and September	Trip on the Concord and Merrimack Rivers with brother John; also to Crawford Notch and the summit of Mt. Washington (pp. 88-93).
1842	July	Walks to Mt. Wachusett with Richard Fuller (p. 132).
1843	May to December	Staten Island; by boat from New London, Conn., to New York City; tutors William Emerson's sons; a second trip to secure his belongings (pp. 145-56).
1844	July and August	Walks alone to Mt. Monadnock and Mt. Greylock; with William Ellery Channing, Jr., visits the Catskill Mts. via a Hudson River boat (pp. 171-72).
1846	August and September	First trip to Maine woods; by rail and boat to Bangor; climbs Mt. Ktaadn; returns to Boston by boat (pp. 208-10).
1848	Summer	With Channing, a walking tour through southern N. H.; Mt. Uncannunuc, Goffstown, Hooksett, Hampstead, and Plaistow (p. 234).
1848	November and December	Lectures in Salem and Gloucester, Mass. (pp. 236-38).
1849	February to April	Lyceum lectures in Salem, Mass.; Portland, Maine; and Worcester, Mass. (pp. 238-42).
1849	October	First trip to Cape Cod; with Channing, via Cohasset and Sandwich; return from Provincetown to Boston on steamer *Naushon* (pp. 270-72).
1850	Spring	Surveying in Haverhill, Mass. (p. 274).
1850	June	Alone to Cape Cod; steamer from Boston to Provincetown and return (pp. 273-74).
1850	July	Fire Island, N. Y.; to aid the search for Margaret Fuller's manuscripts and belongings (pp. 277-79).

[*] This listing excludes all trips made in the immediate vicinity of Concord and Boston. Page references are to Walter Harding's *The Days of Henry Thoreau* (New York, 1965), where fuller descriptions of the trips may be found.

1850	September	Railway excursion to Canada; train to Burlington, Vt.; steamer on Lake Champlain; steamer *John Munn* from Montreal to Quebec and return (pp. 279-81).
1850	December	Lecture at Newburyport, Mass. (p. 285).
1851	January	Lectures at Clinton and Medford, Mass. (p. 285).
1851	May	Lecture at Worcester, Mass. (p. 286).
1851	July and August	Walking trip on the South Shore of Mass.; Hull to Plymouth and Clark's Island; return via Boston (pp. 293-94).
1852	February	Lecture at Plymouth, Mass. (p. 286).
1852	May	Lecture at Plymouth; explores nearby ponds (p. 286).
1852	September	With Channing to Peterboro, Mass. and Mt. Monadnock; return by train from Troy, N. H. (pp. 294-95).
1853	April	Surveying for 17 days in Haverhill, Mass. (p. 326).
1853	September	Second trip to Maine; steamer *Penobscot* to Bangor; Moosehead Lake and Penobscot River; return by steamer *Boston* from Bangor (pp. 309-12).
1853	October	Surveying in Plymouth, Mass. (p. 326).
1853	November	Littleton, Mass., to bring Bulkeley Emerson home for his mother's funeral (p. 302).
1854	October	Train to Westminster, Mass. with H. G. O. Blake and Thomas Cholmondeley; walk to Mt. Wachusett (p. 347). Lecture in Plymouth (p. 341).
1854	November	Train to Philadelphia to lecture; return via New York City (p. 342).
1854	December	Lecture in Providence, R. I. (p. 342). New Bedford to lecture and to visit Daniel Ricketson; steamer from Hyannis to Nantucket Island (pp. 343-45).
1855	January	Lecture in Worcester, Mass. (p. 345).
1855	July	With Channing to Cape Cod; schooner *Melrose* from Boston to Provincetown; return from Provincetown on *Olata* (pp. 359-60).
1855	September	New Bedford to visit Ricketson; explores Middleborough and Fairhaven; return by train from Plymouth (p. 362).
1856	June	One week in Worcester visiting friends (p. 366). New Bedford to visit Ricketson; carriage to Freetown and Fairhaven; steamer *Eagle Wing* to Naushon in the Elizabeth Islands (pp. 367-68).
1856	September	Train to Fitchburg; walks to Westminster; train to Brattleboro, Vt.; explores Connecticut River and Mt. Wantastiquet; train to Bellows Falls; climbs Fall Mountain; wagon to Walpole, N. H. for a visit with Bronson Alcott (pp. 368-70).

1856	October and November	Train and boat to New York City, via Worcester; then to Perth Amboy, N. J. for surveying job at "Eagleswood"; train to Horace Greeley's farm in Westchester, N. Y.; return to Brooklyn for a visit with Walt Whitman (pp. 370-74).
1856	December	Lecture in Amherst, N. H. (pp. 376-77).
1857	February	Lectures in Fitchburg and Worcester, Mass. (p. 377).
1857	April	New Bedford to visit Ricketson (pp. 378-79).
1857	June	Last trip to Cape Cod; train to Plymouth; visits Clark's Island, Manomet Point, Salt Pond, and Scusset; train to Sandwich; walks to Highland Light and Provincetown; steamer *Acorn* to Boston (pp. 382-85).
1857	July and August	Last trip to Maine woods: train to Portland, steamer to Bangor; Allegash and East Branch; train to Portland and night boat to Boston (pp. 385-90).
1858	January	Lecture at Lynn; visits Nahant and Danvers (pp. 395-96).
1858	May	Via Worcester, to New York City on family business; visits Staten Island (pp. 396-97).
1858	June	Train to Troy, N. H.; walks with Blake to Mt. Monadnock (pp. 398-402).
1858	July	With Edward Hoar, by carriage to the White Mts.; climbs Mt. Washington (pp. 398-402).
1858	September	Walking trip on the North Shore of Mass.; Salem, Marblehead, Beverly, Gloucester, Cape Ann (pp. 402-3).
1859	February	Lecture at Worcester (p. 413).
1859	April	Lecture at Lynn; walks on the North Shore (p. 414).
1859	November	Lecture at Worcester (p. 419).
1860	August	Train to Troy, N. H.; walks to Mt. Monadnock with Channing (pp. 431-33).
1860	September	Lecture at Lowell, Mass.; explores Merrimack and lower Concord Rivers (p. 437).
1860	October	Boxboro, Mass. to inspect "Inches Woods" (p. 440).
1860	December	Lecture at Waterbury, Conn. (p 441).
1861	May to July	Minnesota journey; train to Dunleith; steamer *Itasca* up the Mississippi River to St. Paul; steamer *Frank Steele* up the Minnesota River to Redwood; return by riverboat *War Eagle* to Prairie du Chien; train to Milwaukee; steamer *Edith* to Mackinaw City; *Sun* to Goderich, Ontario; train via Ogdensburg, N.Y., to Concord (pp. 444-51).
1861	August	New Bedford to visit Ricketson (pp. 452-53).

Index

THE following index allows readers to locate most of Thoreau's geographical references on the maps in this *Gazetteer*. The index was drawn from a master list of more than 3,000 place names appearing in Thoreau's published works. Researchers were careful to list only those places Thoreau was known to have visited. The master list was then checked against place names on the *Gazetteer* maps, and location symbols were added. Some of the maps contain reference grids, in which cases map numbers appear with coordinates (e.g., 18:H-7).

It should be stressed that this is an index of Thoreau's *writings*, and not just of the *Gazetteer*. Those names on the maps which do not appear in the writings have not been indexed. Conversely, some names appear in the index which are not on the maps. In those instances, notably for the Concord area, conjectural locations appear in brackets [ ]. Numbers in parentheses ( ) correspond to numbers on Gleason's map of Concord, Map 18.

52